CLASSIC NUDE
PHOTOGRAPHY

Techniques
and Images

PETER GOWLAND & ALICE GOWLAND

AMHERST MEDIA, INC. ■ BUFFALO, NY

Published by:
Amherst Media, Inc.
P.O. Box 586
Buffalo, N.Y. 14226
Fax: 716-874-4508
www.AmherstMedia.com

Publisher: Craig Alesse
Senior Editor/Production Manager: Michelle Perkins
Assistant Editor: Barbara A. Lynch-Johnt
Assistant Editor: Matthew Kreib
Scanning Technician: Christopher Boehm

ISBN: 1-58428-040-9
Library of Congress Card Catalog Number: 00-132627

Printed in Korea.
10 9 8 7 6 5 4 3 2 1

INTRODUCTION

ABOUT THE AUTHORS

Before he got behind the camera and set the tone for a generation of glamour photographers, Peter Gowland was in front of it. At the age of six weeks, he made his film debut in *A Small Magnetic Hand*, a movie written by his mother, actress and screenwriter Beatrice Bird. His father, Gibson Gowland, was also an actor (noted for his starring role in Eric Von Stronheim's epic film *Greed*). By the time he was in high school (with classmates Judy Garland and Mickey Rooney), Peter Gowland was working on his lighting techniques as an engineer for school plays.

In the years that followed, he pursued his own acting career, appearing as a bit player, dancer and extra in such films as *Twenty Thousand Leagues Under the Sea*, and the MGM musicals *Born to Dance* and *The Great Ziegfeld*. He even appeared as a stunt double for Ronald Reagan. "I was jumping into a hay cart as a double for Reagan during his first WWII film," says Gowland, noting, "I never listed it on my actor's resume because I felt no one would know who Reagan was."

Gowland's acting career was the starting point for his career in photography, and the lessons learned there have impacted his work ever since. "Both of them (glamour photography and Hollywood films) deal with fantasy," he says. "Another commonality is promotion. The success of Hollywood and my career as a glamour photographer rely on the same promotion philosophy for making themselves well known. Another connection is technical. I learned a lot about how cameras are made and operated in Hollywood."

During his years in film, Gowland supplemented his income snapping candids of fellow actors and taking pictures of starlets (often in his living room), then selling them to movie magazines. "**I knew a lot of beautiful women (on the various sets). I'd work about two days a week and take pictures the rest of the time,**" he says.

In 1941, Peter Gowland met Alice Adams—and married her in Las Vegas on their second date. The couple has been living and working together ever since, in a partnership Peter Gowland credits as invaluable to his success as a photographer. At first, though, Alice frowned on Peter's hobby of photographing women. That was, until she sent the photographs to a couple of magazines and received $200 for each shot. "That was a staggering amount of money in those days," she notes.

In 1946, when Peter returned home from military service, the couple built their first studio with a G.I. Bill loan and began photographing anything they were paid for—cats, babies, homes. By this time, they also had two young daughters (Ann and Mary Lee), and a growing catalog of glamour photography. Thanks to Alice's strong business sense, they sold increasing numbers of images to magazines and calendars. Eventually, they were able to focus on glamour photography. Says Peter, "If I had any success, I think it was because of Alice. She kept me straight."

Gowland's style—depicting tan, athletic California girls—found solid ground in a market hungry for provocative images. Yet, while his images are provocative, they also possess a certain innocence. Says Gowland, "I try to make a nude look like she's got clothes on. Instead of lighting the model, I light the background so that she's silhouetted and clothed in shadow. **I prefer to cover, and glamorize and make things exciting.**"

Over the years, Peter Gowland's glamour photography earned over 1000 magazine covers. He was one of the first photographers to submit work to *Playboy*, which eventually featured his photographs in nine centerfolds and on several covers. "I can remember in those days," recalls Peter, "[Hugh] Hefner would call me up on a Sunday morning to check on the pictures. There was a very personal feeling about being involved with that magazine at the time." Gowland's work was also featured in advertising for Black Velvet, Smirnoff Vodka, Lancer's Wine, Polaroid, Kodak, GE, NBC and many others. Since 1964, the couple has also produced the photographs for the Ridge Tool Company calendar.

However, glamour photography is only one facet of the Gowland story. As it happened, Alice also had a flair for writing and turned it into an inventive sales method soon after the opening of their first studio. "My wife and I are a good combination," says Peter, "When I met her, I didn't realize she had such talent. I just thought she was cute." Pairing text with photos, they produced stories for the *L.A. Times*, *L.A. Home* magazine and *Better Homes and Gardens*. In 1954, they wrote their first book—an instructional volume entitled *How to Photograph Women* (Crown). Over twenty books would follow.

From 1942-44, Peter also served as a photographer for North American Aviation. Later, he applied some of the techniques used in aircraft design to building his own lightweight cameras. It is a pursuit about which he remains passionate. To date, Gowland has invented 23 large format cameras and numerous pieces of movie equipment used by Kodak, Polaroid, *Life*, and the FBI. His most famous camera, the custom-made Gowlandflex, has been owned by celebrated photographers Yousef Karsh and Philippe Halsman. He still produces his custom cameras—now marketing them on his web site (petergowland.com). It doesn't make him rich, he says, but the fun and variety make it worth the time he spends.

Looking back on their career to date—including photographing the biggest stars of Hollywood (James Garner, Alfred Hitchcock, Jayne Mansfield and Raquel Welch to name a very few), and setting the standard for glamour photography for years to come—neither of the Gowlands is ready to rest on their laurels. **Retirement is not a word in their vocabulary, says the couple.** Besides which, "retiring" would imply that the last fifty years had been spent working, something Peter denies. "We love what we do," he states simply. "I feel like I have never worked. I may have worked, but I don't ever remember working. Photography has always been play."

INTRODUCTION

Photography, for me, was a sideline to working as an extra in the movie business, when I met Alice, 58 years ago. I'd been trying to get into the Cinematographers' Union but had no family connections in that area, but my father, Gibson Gowland, was an actor, so I was able to get into the Actors' Union. It was my photography that brought Alice and I together. Her boyfriend was an acquaintance of mine. He wanted pictures of her. That's how we met. **We married on our second date!**

Alice had the idea that we could supplement our income by selling pictures, freelance, to magazines and calendars, but I wasn't so sure. I told her about selling a picture layout on the Hollywood Studio Club, a residence for aspiring actresses and professional women, and how it went through two agents, each taking a chunk of the money and leaving me with barely enough to pay for the film. **That made Alice even more determined.** "We'll do it on our own," she said, even though she knew nothing about how she would do it. We began with color pictures of our adorable, blue-eyed baby daughter, Ann; petting

Models never came between them, but the Gowlandflex camera became his mistress. That was hard for Alice to take.

a kitty, eating cookies, or just smiling. Alice sent them off to a company whose name she found on the back of a calendar and that was the beginning.

Together we've taken over 100,000 photographs. Of these, only a small percentage are nudes. Most were a creative outlet, rather than on assignment. Our main source of income has always been through advertising accounts where Art Directors have influenced the results. We were able to publish the nude work throughout the 24 books we've written on the subject of photography, usually only 25 percent of each book.

We've selected our favorite sixty images and it has been a happy experience living with these negatives for the last few months. Happy, because it took us back to the very day we shot the pictures and what a pleasure it was.

Together we've taken over 100,000 photographs. Of these, only a small percentage are nudes. Most of these were a creative outlet, rather than on assignment.

Window Light

SIMPLICITY

I like the simplicity of window light. Maybe that's why I'm drawn to Rembrandt paintings. For the novice photographer it's a good beginning because, usually, no additional lighting is necessary. When using window light, you are down to basics with no need for stands, wires, reflectors—only your camera and tripod.

There are two types of window light: direct, hard sun and indirect, soft light. Each give a different effect. **This portrait of Joan Slemmons is a good example of hard sun used to advantage.**

The image was created using light from the ceiling-to-floor glass window in my studio. Direct rays from the sun came from camera right. **They accentuate the curve of Joan's small breasts** by defining them with dark shadows.

Joan's face is turned profile, because the harsh shadows, as on the body, would be unflattering to her face.

Exposure was for sunlight, as though outdoors. In this case, it was 1/125th at f/16, using Verichrome Pan.

I like the simplicity of window light. Maybe that's why I'm drawn to Rembrandt paintings.

Joan Slemmons, 1955

AUTHENTICITY

Martie Lacher has a fresh, youthful face and petite figure so we thought of her in a candid situation rather than a classic nude study.

We asked Martie to assume a pose by the glass window in the office of our studio/home. The availability of an authentic home atmosphere is one advantage to a combination studio/ home workplace.

The sun is hitting Martie from a high angle and only falls on half of her body, missing her face entirely, which creates a softer facial image than direct sun as with Joan Slemmons (previous page). The parts of Martie's body missed by the sun are illuminated by opening up the

The availability of an authentic home atmosphere is one advantage to a combination studio/home workplace.

camera lens two stops to accommodate the low ambient lighting of the room. **By doing this, part of the breast area, that lit by the sun, is overexposed.** But, we felt it made a better overall picture than bringing in extra lights, which would take away from the natural look.

Martie Lacher, 1968

Soft Lighting

In my sixty years of photographing models, Patti is one of my favorite models. She is not too tall, short, thin or fat but is perfectly proportioned. It's not necessary to stick to certain angles of face or body, since she photographs well from all angles.

A friend's house provided this lovely window seat with paned glass and foliage outside. No sun came through the windows except at the far right corner.

We preferred to have Patti facing the window, which cast a soft lighting to her torso and profile. **This left a dark area in the center of her body, while the brighter side edged the shape of her leg and part of her arm.** No additional equipment was necessary.

We used a Hasselblad with an 80mm lens (normal) and Verichrome Pan film, developed in Kodak D-76.

Patti Connelly, 1960

Debra Ghaske, 1986

ON LOCATION

We watched a new home being built near ours and were fascinated by the structure. I introduced myself to the owner, and he proudly showed me through. I knew when I saw the circular window over a white bed in an all-white room with one bright red anthurium in a simple vase, that I had to photograph a nude figure in that setting. Later, I telephoned the owner and asked if I could photograph a model in his home and he said yes.

Debra Ghaske, a dancer, came to mind immediately. She had come to us in need of photographs before we saw this house. I remembered that her figure was the type we like and felt she would be perfect for the location.

Later, I telephoned the owner and asked if I could photograph a model in his home and he said yes.

Outside greenery filled the round glass area. By having Debra look outside, with her hair piled on top of her head, the beautiful neckline and curves of her lithe body became the focal point of the setting.

In back of the camera the entire wall was glass. **This still was not bright enough to compensate for the additional amount of light that she looked into.** Overexposure was necessary in order to attain good skin tones on Debra, and this caused the greenery to lose some of its richness. However, the lighter, faded tones seemed even more appropriate for the setting.

Marli Renfru had no trouble posing because she is an accomplished dancer and had posed for artists. **She has a natural dramatic sense of her body language.**

Marli Renfru
had no
trouble posing
because
she is an
accomplished
dancer and
had posed
for artists.

This photograph was shot against a white seamless paper roll, nine feet wide, which hung from the background wall of our studio.

Marli is seated on an antique chair, inherited from my mother. She did not appreciate that I removed one leg to make it like a tripod. **Not seen in the photo is a full-length mirror on casters, next to the camera.** In that way, Marli was able to direct herself.

A ceiling-to-floor, diffused glass window at the right was the only illumination for the photograph, which is one of my all-time favorites. This is partially because of the S-curve body shape Marli was able to accomplish, and the dramatic tilt of her head and open lips.

POSING

Marli Renfru, 1961

We photographed Candace on a number of occasions, both as a pinup and as a nude. She was always fun to be with and enjoyed working out poses that had a bit more zip than the classic nude studies.

This photograph was created in our daylight studio on a white paper roll hung against our curved wall.

A ceiling-to-floor, diffused glass window was located to Candace's right. Exposure varies in this situation, depending on the time and type of day. No additional lighting was used.

This photograph was created in our daylight studio on a white paper roll hung against our curved wall.

Candace Thayer (a.k.a. Candace Elkins), 1968

AUGMENTED WINDOW LIGHT

This photograph was taken in our daylight studio near the floor-to-ceiling window.

Judy was a young actress who added to her income by doing a limited amount of figure photography. While I don't usually have my nude models looking into the camera, Judy's personality, along with her pretty features and coquettish expression, seemed to fit with the pose. Notice that all of the models in this book have natural breasts—no implants.

The light from the window was augmented by the use of a single flood next to camera left. We felt this was necessary because I was not trying for a classic nude study, but rather a more intimate sexy image. **We faced Judy's body toward the window and had her twist slightly so that the right breast covers the gap between the two, thus accentuating their perfect symmetry.**

Judy Crowder, 1959

23

Simple Sunlight

EXPOSURE

Susanne is a nudist who shares our feeling that the human body is a thing of beauty and mystery. She practices good health in all of life's aspects and it shows in the glow of her skin and her trim figure. She has an innate ability to pose gracefully whether in action or still.

This image was created at Susanne's Zuma Beach home, with easy access to the water at 7 a.m. The sun had just risen low on the horizon. Its reflection in the water was so bright that I had to reduce the exposure, thus making sunlight look like moonlight.

In order not to leave a mark on the wet sand, **Susanne assumed this difficult pose as the wave came to shore and held it as the water receded.** A star filter added sparkle to the sun's reflection.

Its reflection in the water was so bright that I had to reduce the exposure, thus making sunlight look like moonlight.

Susanne Severeid, 1981

BACKGROUNDS

There's an advantage to working with a nude outdoors with basic sunlight in that no additional equipment is necessary. I look for plain backgrounds such as, in this case, a small sand dune. It was shielded from public view, but we still had to watch for police or lifeguards because of the ban on nudity in public areas. That added a bit of excitement, but did not interfere with our enthusiasm.

The shadows cast on a figure using basic sunlight will vary depending on the time of day. Here, we're working at noon, a time we avoid for bathing suit pictures where the model is looking into the camera because we prefer the sun to back-light her.

Joann situated her body on the slant of the dune, thus letting more sun fall on her figure. I asked her to tip her head back to prevent her eyes from becoming dark pits.

I look for plain backgrounds, as in this case, a small sand dune.

Joann Arnold, 1950

Melodi
held up
a used
fishnet
that we
found on
the beach.

This photograph was made at Malibu beach, about a half a mile north of Paradise Cove in Southern California. Photographing anyone nude in public is prohibited and subject to a heavy fine. **Today it is more difficult than ever to try to find secluded beaches**—particularly in Malibu, where homes above the cliffs can easily see what goes on. When this picture was taken, the area did not have such dense housing. By getting up early, we were able to work free from prying eyes.

Simple sunlight with no reflector or electronic flash was used for this photograph. Melodi held up a used fishnet that we found on the beach. **With the net between her torso and the sun, dramatic shadows were cast across her body.**

This image falls into my Rolleiflex years—from 1938 to 1955. I loved my fourteen Rolleis, but discovered the Hasselblad could change lenses and change backs, enabling me to switch with ease between shooting in black & white and color. I could also use a Polaroid back for quick testing.

However, to give credit where credit is due, the over 600 4"x5" Gowlandflex cameras (my own model) that we have made and sold, are the result of my appreciation for the twin-lens Rolleiflex.

Melodi Lowell, 1951

Ann Cushing's body was perfection; even her hands and feet were beautifully shaped. She was a pleasure to work with.

This photograph was made a one-half mile walk North

of Paradise Cove, where high cliffs supported private residences. The homes were far enough back that we didn't worry about being seen.

We had hoped to use color film at sunrise, but the weather did not cooperate. Instead, we had heavy mist and it was cold. Foggy backgrounds have never appealed to me, so it was only Ann's courage and unwillingness to give up that sparked my spirit.

Alice had brought along this one-of-a-kind hat, made by a designer friend, Jo Lathwood, who was known for her beachwear. I liked its shape and having Ann's pretty face hidden added to the candidness of the picture. In the end, this was my favorite pose of the day.

> We had hoped to use color film at sunrise, but the weather did not cooperate.

WEATHER

This image was photographed on the patio connected to our studio/home. Diane is lying next to the pool coping.

The photograph was lit with sunlight—around 1 p.m. on a warm day. Ordinarily, I would use a strobe fill, but because this is a nude, I prefer the strong shadows. **In this instance, they are not unflattering to her pensive expression.**

Diane was a favorite model, and more photographs of her are featured in a later chapter.

Ordinarily,
I would use
a strobe fill,
but because
this is a
nude, I
prefer
the strong
shadows.

Diane Webber, 1951

Studio

OFFBEAT POSES

Experimenting with offbeat poses can result in unique images, such as this one. It was taken with the model lying on a soft, white rug, in our white studio. Later, Virgin Island Airlines bought the use of the picture for advertising their "Flight to the Virgins."

One light was used from each side, creating the shadow areas in the middle.

Experimenting with offbeat poses can result in unique images such as this one.

Anonymous, 1969

This photograph of Brooke was made in our home/studio in Rustic Canyon (between Santa Monica and Malibu), California. **The white, sixteen foot wide shooting wall is curved at both the ceiling and the floor.** It connects directly with the white terrazzo floor. This setup is particularly good for photographing dancers. They can make leaps without worry of a line at the ceiling or floor. The result is a consistently clean, white background to the figure.

> This setup is particularly good for photographing dancers.

Three lights were used on Brooke. The key light was placed to the left of the camera, while the background light was placed to camera right (making sure this flood didn't hit the shadow side of the model). The third light was a spotlight used over the model on a boom to accent the model's hair.

For this image, I used my favorite $2^{1}/_{4}$x$2^{1}/_{4}$ camera, the Hasselblad 500C, with an 80mm lens. The film used was Kodak Verichrome, developed in D-76.

SHOOTING AREA

At the time this photograph was taken I did not have a commercial studio, but converted my living room into a small shooting area by moving furniture.

The Hollywood Studio Club was located near the California bungalow that I rented at the time. **Lee Evans was a serious dancer who lived there along with other performers and career women.** She had never done any nude modeling and since I was looking for a pretty model to expand my photography, I asked her to pose. She was shy, but appreciated art and so agreed.

I concocted a platform onto which I threw a lambs' wool rug. I placed one floodlight on the floor, in back of Lee, pointed up against the white wall. Another flood was mounted on a stand, placed high, to camera right.

The setup was completed with a mirror, taken off the wall and propped up next to the camera to aid the model in posing. At this point, Lee asked that I leave the room, saying she would pose herself and, when ready, would call me.

During the session, I used a 4"x5" Graflex camera with sheet film and only made about five exposures. **We were both surprised that the picture turned out so well.** In fact, it's one of my favorites. If I were doing the shoot today, however, I would have used backlighting on her hair.

On a sad note, we feel that our filing system is good and we rarely lose or misplace a negative. This one is the unfortunate exception; it has been missing for years.

I concocted
a platform
onto
which
I threw
a lambs'
wool rug.

Lee Evans, 1940

I prefer to photograph the figure with shadows in mind, showing the outline of the body in high contrast to the background.

By now you must recognize that I keep technique simple: background, lighting and props. I prefer to photograph the figure with shadows in mind, showing the outline of the body in high contrast to the background. **In this instance, only one light was used.** It was placed to camera left, aimed mainly at the background but with enough "spill" to edge-light Margie's profile and breasts.

Placement of the light is more important than the type of light used. I defy anyone to tell me if this photograph was made with electronic flash or floods. Floods can be hot to work under, and yet bright for focusing and for seeing just where the shadows will fall. Electronic flash can be expensive and the pilot lights are weak, making it difficult to see the exact shadow pattern.

As a side note, Margie Harrison had a serious scar on the calf of one leg that could have disqualified her for some photographers, but it made the sitting more of a challenge to both of us. She appreciated the beauty of the photographs afterwards.

Margie Harrison, 1951

POSING

Linda was able to configure her body in almost any shape. **Her dance background made her limber and graceful.** She needed very little encouragement in originating poses that I'd never seen before. This one is one of my favorites.

The key light came from camera right but was turned more toward the background, with fewer rays striking Linda's figure. I added a second light to camera left. This was directed entirely onto the background to separate her profile in a silhouette image.

Linda was
able to
configure
her body
in almost
any
shape.

Linda York, 1973

The building of this hot tub is described in a later section on using water in photography. In that case, it was used with a black background. Here, one light on either side of Gayna was directed onto a light background. It created an early morning effect.

Gayna was standing more erect when I asked her to bend, because I don't like stick figure compositions. By leaning forward with her arm back, three triangles are formed—two between her arms and body and one between her legs. **This fills the frame of the picture, making it more pleasing to the eye.**

By leaning forward with her arm back, three triangles are formed.

Gayna Reed, 1979

Melody Ward, 1957

The backdrop for this photograph was the white wall of the studio, with fern fronds attached to the light stands. Two lights were used. One was placed on each side of the model, but directed mainly toward the background.

The amount of detail in the figure depends on two things: how close to the background the light is placed, and how much is turned toward the model in relationship to how much is turned onto the background.

It helps to have an assistant who can move the lights while you look from the camera's angle. I usually take a Polaroid, as I find it will save time in the long run.

It helps
to have
an assistant
who can
move
the lights
while you
look from
the camera's
angle.

DETAIL

Dramatic

Candace Thayer (a.k.a. Candace Elkins), 1968

A Simple Setup

We photographed this image outdoors. The background was created by propping a framed 6'x6' square of black felt against the sliding glass doors of our patio. The "hammock," is actually a piece of net cloth we purchased at a local yardage store. We tied it to two roof-support posts.

The part of the patio where we created the setup is under a five foot overhang of the house. It was a sunny day but, because of the overhang, no sun fell directly on this area. **We used shaded daylight only, with no reflectors.**

We photographed Candace on several occasions and always found her to be a natural at posing.

The "hammock," is actually a piece of net cloth we purchased at a local yardage store.

Margie Harrison, 1951

Using dark backgrounds gives a chance to play with backlighting and create dramatic effects.

Using dark backgrounds gives a chance to play with backlighting and create dramatic effects. We prefer a black cloth rather than paper roll because the cloth absorbs more light, and does not reflect as the paper does at times.

We borrowed this antique bench from a friend. **Margie posed with one floodlight from each side.** The light at camera right was directed toward her from the background, while the one at camera left was immediately to the side of her.

BACKLIGHTING

FEET TOWARD THE CAMERA

Photographing legs in this position, with the feet toward the camera, is tricky because feet are not the most photogenic part of the body. It works here because we hid them with partial shading.

For this photograph, two backlights were used. The one to camera left was bare. The other, to camera right, was diffused.

The model was posed in the studio on a raised platform covered in black cloth and set against a black cloth background.

Photographing legs in this position, with the feet toward the camera, is tricky.

Chris Rose, 1973

Back in the '70s, we seemed to get numerous requests for stock photographs of girls with guns, so we decided to incorporate several into our file. Tina Hedgrin was a young, aspiring actress, who needed new photographs for her portfolio, so she agreed to the sitting.

This real-looking gun is actually a toy! In order to create a smoking gun, we dropped a lit cigarette into the barrel.

At first glance, this photograph looks as though the lighting is my usual "simple" arrangement. However, two strobes acted as backlights, augmented by the use of a third, diffused strobe from camera right. The top of Tina's hat was rimmed by a hairlight placed high to camera left.

This
real-looking
gun is
actually
a toy!

Tina Hedgrin, 1978

Water

Joann Arnold, 1950

UNDERWATER

Anyone who follows my photography knows that I am almost obsessed with water. To me, this ever-changing substance is a source of endless possibilities when photographing anything—and particularly women. For years, I had imagined the image of a beautiful figure underwater but **in the '50s, underwater pictures were rare, especially those of women.**

I didn't know of any underwater cameras, so I built a watertight box of plywood with glass on top and on one side. Then I rented an aqua lung, which enabled me to submerge in a friend's pool.

This was a first experience for both Joann and me. I asked her to submerge after me and strike a graceful pose. What surprised us was the effect of the sunlight against the walls of the pool.

While I was photographing Joann Arnold on my first time underwater, **I was immediately struck by the many variations of reflections possible.** Here, her body is underwater and her face is just barely above the surface.

By aiming the camera at the top surface with Joann's head above, her body and face are distorted, but in a provocative way. I had her expel air through her nose and mouth just before the exposure was made, thus creating the bubbles.

The natural sunlight through the water creates a shadow pattern on Joann's body.

Here,
her body is
underwater
and her
face is
barely
above the
surface.

Joann Arnold, 1950

REFLECTIONS

This photograph was created on the white, terrazzo floor of the studio during an evening shoot.

I had become interested in the reflected surface of the terrazzo floor and realized it could be emphasized if it were wet. **I carefully poured one-eighth inch of water onto the surface for the shoot.**

I had taken many dancing photographs of Alison and talked to her about the possibility of modeling for the wet terrazzo idea. She was excited and thought it would be an interesting experiment.

One strobe light from each side of the model was directed onto the background—a curved wall that connects with the white floor. This created a silhouette effect, and the water provided the reflected image.

At first, Alison assumed a side-reclining pose. As we kept working with the idea, we soon found that lying flat, with her back arched and legs bent, created a more interesting design. It may look simple and relaxed, but the arched back and tipped head required the endurance and strength that only a dancer can provide. What amazed me most was Alison's willingness to put her head in the cold water.

This created a silhouette effect, and the water provided the reflected image.

Alison Charie, 1980

Once I had found the reflected wet-background technique, I tried the experiment with other dancers. Linda York, a petite dancer, did a series of poses on the wet terrazzo.

For this photograph, one strobe light was positioned on either side of the model. These lights were directed onto the white curved wall background, with just enough "spilling" onto her body to keep it from becoming a black silhouette.

For this photograph, one strobe light was positioned on either side of the model.

Linda York, 1973

FURTHER REFLECTIONS

This artificial hot tub was built in my studio by placing a sheet of black plastic on the floor and forming blocks of wood in a circle on top of it. The plastic and blocks were held together by a strip of thin plywood. On the front, which is not really shown in the photographs, the plastic was brought up and anchored over the blocks by clips. **We then poured warm water up to three inches.**

Two strobe lights are directed onto the model, one from each side, thus stopping the action of the water stream and the crystal patterns of the drops.

The plastic and blocks were held together by a strip of thin plywood.

Gayna Reed, 1979

Props

CHAIRS

Candace, being a dancer, was always good for an unusual pose. I believe it was Alice who suggested Candace straddle this antique cane rocker. **Candace had no trouble in accomplishing the uncomfortable position.** We saved this pose until last because of the markings that the chair made on Candace's body.

The photograph was taken with light from a ceiling-to-floor window at camera right. A single light was directed on the seamless, curved wall in back of model, camera left, to separate her from the background.

Candace Thayer, 1968

Chairs have a character all their own. They've always been a favorite prop of mine. For nude studies they make a perfect companion both because of their appearance, and because they aid the

Chairs have a character all their own. They've always been a favorite prop of mine.

model in posing. I look for chairs with a sense of line and form (which is what I look for in a model as well). For example, I have never used an overstuffed piece of furniture in a picture (or an overstuffed model).

I let the model decide how she plans to use the prop. In this case, I did wait until the end of the sitting for Colleen to actually sit on the modern, wired piece. Otherwise, it could have turned her body into a tic-tac-toe game!

A four strobe setup, with two on each side, was directed primarily onto the background, but partially hitting the model. The photograph was taken with a Hasselblad and 80mm lens on Verichrome Pan film.

MORE ON CHAIRS

Hat and Chair

A friend's garden and wicker chair provided a nice setting for this model, with the broad-brimmed hat as an additional prop.

The model saw immediately that this chair lent itself to having the body in it rather than standing beside it. Notice how her shape conforms so easily to the shape of the chair. **In art, the student is always searching for the S-curve.** Here, the model definitely has it.

Both the model and the chair were in the shade, illuminated by a silver reflector from the camera's position. The overexposed background created a clear area for the main part of the photograph; the chair and model.

The image was taken on a Hasselblad camera, using an 80mm lens and Verichrome Pan film, developed in D-76.

A friend's garden and wicker chair provided a nice setting for this model.

Anonymous, 1963

Action

Linda York, 1973

THE DANCING NUDE

I depend on the model's personality and attitude to avoid poses that might expose private areas of her body—particularly with action. Linda York, a graceful dancer had a good sense of herself and an appreciation for humor. She understood immediately when I explained that her body would be partially in shadow, and that poses should be rehearsed. **She avoided the stock leaps and twirls and invented this capricious pose.**

A white, seamless paper roll, nine feet wide, served as the backdrop. Window light coming from camera right was assisted by a single photoflood at camera left. This was aimed at the background to wash out the shadow of the model's figure and to separate her from the background.

Window light coming from camera right was assisted by a single photo flood at camera left.

73

WHIMSICAL POSES

Pat is another artist who enjoys spontaneous and whimsical poses rather than classic, sophisticated body language.

Window light illuminated the model from the ceiling-to-floor window at camera right. A floodlight was used to the left of the camera.

Pat is another artist who enjoys spontaneous and whimsical poses rather than classic, sophisticated body language. **Instead of sitting on the woven ottoman, she decided to roll on it.**

Pat was photographed against the curved white plastered wall of the studio, which appears in many other photographs in this book. Instead of shooting on the terrazzo floor, a nubby textured rug was laid down on the floor.

Pat Williams, 1963

Joanne Carroll, 1954

This photograph was taken in my first commercial studio, built with a G.I. loan in 1947.

This oversized lantern appealed to both Joanne and me. She is an artist who likes to find new creative outlets. **We both felt that including it in the photograph was overdoing the scene, but we left it in anyway.**

I built the framework, seen in the background, in my garage/workshop and covered it with diffused plastic. We placed a light behind it, directed at Joanne's waist. Another light, inside the lantern, created the same edge light to the curve of her breast, in front.

I built the
framework
in my
garage/workshop
and covered
it with
diffused
plastic.

PROPS

There is nothing new about using hair to create a feeling of motion. Every glamour photographer I know has made an image of a model with her hair flying. **This doesn't need to stop a novice from trying his hand at it.** In fact, he could come up with something quite different and original.

I had done the flipping of wet hair and the twisting of the head, but since Joy was an energetic dancer, I asked her first to strike a pose that might denote action. Then I asked her to hang her head down and flip it up, maintaining her original position. We didn't have to make many exposures to get this striking picture.

Four lights were positioned to hit the background. Enough light bounces off it to give a minimum of detail to her breasts and derriere.

I added the philodendron leaves because of the similarity in shape to Joy's flying hair.

We didn't have to make many exposures to get this striking picture.

Joy Langstaff, 1952

ADDING ACTION

I asked Shelly to pose on hands and knees like an animal—I didn't specify which animal. **The static poses were okay, but I wanted a bit of action, so I asked her if she could toss her head.** She amazed me with the energy she mustered to flip her head over and over until we felt we had the shot. In this one, her hair fell into shape like the mane of a lion.

Sunlight, diffused by a frosted glass window to camera right, brightened the front of Shelly's body. The white wall behind her received only a small portion of the sunlight, so it became a gray tone that separated her darkened torso from the background.

Shelly Berman, 1973

I asked Shelly to pose on hands and knees like an animal— I didn't specify which animal.

LIGHTING

Two lights were placed on either side of the model, but directed mainly at the background.

This image of Pat was taken in the studio with white, seamless paper roll as background.

Two lights were placed on either side of the model, but directed mainly at the background. **This gave enough fill light to her body to prevent it from becoming completely dark and losing definition.**

Using the same technique of tossing the head, Pat used this authentic African drum to help her get into the mood for posing.

Pat Williams, 1963

Effects

Patti Connelly, 1960

MIRRORS

This photograph was taken at the home of Robert Weaver Stevens, a successful decorator and personal friend.

The model's image was photographed as reflected in a large antique mirror. **One floodlight was directed onto Patti's back from camera right.** I was using Ektachrome 8x10 with a view camera. For the black and white exposures, I used my Hasselblad. The Polaroid tests were also made with the Hasselblad, since using an 8x10 Polaroid would have been prohibitive.

This photograph was taken as an assignment for a company that sold oil drilling equipment. The idea was to make the photograph look as though Lina were lying in oil from a "gusher" well.

Lina laid on the floor of my studio against a length of black plastic that comes in 54" rolls. Above her, close to the camera were two Larson Reflectasols; one 2000 watt-second 73", set at 1200 watt-seconds, and the other an 800 watt-second 26". These can be seen reflected in the black plastic. By using poetic license, the client accepted the effect as close to what he wanted.

I used 120 Verichrome Pan with my Hasselblad for the test, then switched to 4"x5" Ektachrome on the final pictures.

The idea was to make the photograph look as though Lina were lying in oil from a "gusher" well.

OIL WELL

LITHO FILM

The print
was then
copied on
4"x5" Litho film,
which eliminated
the half-tones
and transformed
the figure
to hard black
and white.

To get away from the standard black and white photograph, I experimented with Lithographic film to copy a negative shot on regular Verichrome Pan. Litho film is too slow (ASA 2 or 10) to stop action. **Even using ASA 100, the indoor exposure with window light was 1/60th of a second, and we had a slight blur.**

Before making any exposures, Virginia went through a series of movements that I studied carefully. I then chose the ones I wanted her to repeat for the actual shooting. We went through the poses several times with an exposure of 1/125th of a second at f/5.6, using window light coming in from the right. A conventional half-tone print was made from our favorites. The print was then copied on 4"x5" Litho film, which eliminated the half-tones and transformed the figure to hard black and white.

Virginia De Lee, 1955

This photograph was created in the counter area of my first commercial studio.

A white paper roll was placed on the counter that ran across the slanted front windows of the studio about four feet above ground level. The paper was then pulled down to extend across the floor. Ronnie would be hidden from public view because she was so close to this outside wall.

We had calculated when the sun would be coming directly through the windows at camera left, then removed some of the display photographs from the window area. These were replaced with a piece of Peg-Board which the sunlight passed through, creating white dots on the floor. **By positioning Ronnie in that area, the pattern covered her as well.** We moved her position several times to make different configurations.

Ronnie would be hidden from public view because she was so close to this outside wall.

PEG-BOARD

Ronnie Scott, 1953

Joy Berman, 1958

LIGHT EFFECTS

This photograph was taken on the floor of a bedroom, next to a set of sliding glass doors. Wall-to-wall carpeting covered the floor. The door was opened for the shoot and a bamboo screen was hung over the area, creating a pattern on Joy's body. **The light from the screen was used without any additional fill light.** Joy's face was turned toward the light in order to capture detail on her pretty face.

Combining Images

Printing two images on the same sheet of paper takes concentration and testing of each negative before either is printed. Alison had first posed for me on the white, terrazzo floor of our studio. We had poured water on it for reflection. I used two different enlargers to make the print because Alison's picture was taken on 4"x5" film and the clouds were on 120 film. If the two pictures you choose are both on the same size film you may use a single enlarger.

1. In the darkroom I placed the 4"x5" negative of Alison in the enlarger and projected it onto a sheet of plain white paper, situated on the easel.

2. I traced the projected outline of Alison's body onto the paper.

3. I then placed a small strip of enlarging paper on top of this.

4. With a piece of cardboard, I blocked off two-thirds of the strip and made a five-second exposure.

5. I moved the cardboard one-half inch and made a second exposure of five seconds.

6. I removed the cardboard and made a third, five-second exposure. I now had three exposures to choose from; five, ten and fifteen seconds.

7. With an exposure selected, I printed the negative on a sheet of enlarging paper.

8. I wrote my technical data on the back. This would also let me know which was the top of the page.

9. I returned it to the light-tight envelope.

10. From my collection of cloud pictures, photographed through a yellow filter, which dramatizes the effect, I selected a $2^{1}/_{4}$ negative.

11. I put this negative into the 2nd enlarger, and made test strips giving me the correct exposure for the cloud negative.

12. I placed the paper sketch on the easel.

13. I moved the easel so that Alison's body was in the confines of the projected cloud image, and not in the sky area.

14. I retrieved the exposed, yet undeveloped sheet from the envelope and carefully placed it on the easel, making sure the top was at the top, then printed the cloud negative over it.

15. I developed the paper and when dried, it was the double-image photograph seen here.

Alison Charie, 1980

Joan Webb, 1958

Joan
leaned
back in
the swing
and I tilted
the camera
to give the
appearance
of her body
in motion.

This image of Joan was created in the studio. **The swing was hung from two hooks in the studio ceiling.** Joan leaned back in the swing and I tilted the camera to give the appearance of her body in motion.

Two lights were used, one to camera left and one to camera right.

This image of Joan was composited with a second photograph using the same procedure as with the photograph of Alison Charie (previous page) except that a different cloud formation, one that included the tops of trees, was used.

SWING

"BUDDY"

Bettina had told me she owned a boa named "Buddy." She carried him to our studio in a paper bag! Using a white paper roll, Bettina went through a series of poses with "Buddy." I had never worked with snakes and didn't think of them as cuddly pets, but Bettina and "Buddy" interacted together much as one would with a cat or dog. **She talked to him, petted him, draped him around her, and held him in the air.**

One light was used on the studio background at camera right. One light was placed at camera left and aimed mainly at the background, but also allowed to "spill" slightly on Bettina's back.

Using the same technique as with the other combined images, I selected an ocean-at-sunset photograph rather than clouds. This was one of the most difficult to print and, in the end, required slight retouching where the waist meets the horizon.

Bettina, 1982

The photograph of model Lesley Heasler was created in the studio with a white paper roll as the background.

One light was positioned at camera left, primarily hitting the background but also spilling over onto the model. Another soft light was placed in front, near the camera.

I've always felt that any kind of foliage is best used as a frame for a photograph of a person, rather than the entire background. **I've taken photographs of different trees for this purpose.** I selected this one, taken on a grassy knoll with plenty of white sky behind it. It seemed to work perfectly with the pose.

I've always felt that any kind of foliage is best used as a frame for a photograph of a person.

Lesley Heasler, 1987

Ann Cushing, 1971

CUTOUT

I wanted to experiment with cutting out a particular image (either black and white or color), and then rephotographing it with a real-life object.

I had photographed Ann Cushing in a series of poses on our studio floor and selected this one as suitable for a glass of champagne. I made a print on double-weight paper, then very carefully cut out the image and placed it in the champagne glass, which was atop a white box, and rephotographed it. I kept the photograph of Ann in place by using a small piece of clay in back of her, out of sight.

One soft-light was used as a key light from camera left. A second light was used on the background.

Diane Webber

Diane Webber, 1955

A FAVORITE MODEL

What I loved about Diane was the creative quality she brought to every photography session. Diane is 5'2", with a curvaceous body. I thought she might appear heavy in photographs but the grace with which she walked—head high, hair piled on top, her feet and hands moving like a dancer, changed my mind. **Once we started working together it became obvious that Diane enjoyed her craft.** She brought a sensitivity and enthusiasm that I had not seen before.

With the help of my assistant I placed a white paper roll on the edge of the roof in the patio area and unrolled it to create a background. We anchored the roll with sandbags on the roof and the extended paper with a couple of bricks. This kind of setup can only be done on a sunny, windless day. We asked Diane to sit on the white, upholstered chair.

Midday sunlight was the only source of illumination. Because I feel the nude figure cries out for shadows, I had to create some in this instance. My assistant held a branch from a Hawaiian tree fern, making sure that Diane's profile was in the clear. The guitar was used as a prop, enabling Diane to lengthen the appearance of her leg by resting it on the curve of the instrument.

What
I loved
about Diane
was the
creative
quality
she brought
to every
photography
session.

Diane Webber, 1955

One
simple
prop is
of great
help in
posing
models.

One simple prop is of great help in posing models whether nude or in clothing. This is the case with the addition of the spidery-legged coffee table to this shot.

Notice that erotic points are hidden by Diane's pose or by shadows. Her face, sensuous in its simple relaxed expression, with eyes closed, is tilted for the most flattering angle of high noon sun.

PROPS

My white studio, with its curved wall that meets the white terrazzo floor, was the setting for this image.

I was fortunate in knowing Robert Weaver Stevens, a talented decorator who graciously loaned me the use of his many pieces of antique furniture, as well as his home. **This gigantic scale, with its alabaster fruit, seemed to me an unlikely prop for Diane.** She loved it, however, and quickly knelt behind it in a whimsical pose.

The key light is a flood directed on Diane from camera left. The second light is a flood directed on the background from camera left. The third light is a floor-to-ceiling diffused glass window to camera right.

She, however, loved it and quickly knelt behind it in a whimsical pose.

Diane Webber, 1955

OVERSIZED PROP

Diane Webber, 1955

She
had no
trouble
with
expressions,
even when
holding
her
breath.

Diane telephoned me to say she was four months pregnant but still able to be photographed. **Realizing this condition could change her forever, I jumped at the chance.**

We decided to work in and around the swimming pool. I used my Rolleiflex in an underwater housing.

What a pleasant surprise to find that Diane was as familiar with posing underwater as above. She had no trouble with expressions, even when holding her breath. She could stay under for five or six exposures. I found I could stay under about a minute and twenty seconds. I would sink to the bottom first, then Diane would slowly come into view and strike a pose or two with the sun casting light patterns against the side of the pool.

When photographing underwater, I like to use color film because I have the option to create both black and white and color prints by copying the 120 color transparency onto a 4"x5" black and white negative.

UNDERWATER

CLEAR WATER

In working with swimming pools, one can add chemicals that assist in settling the fine particles of dust.

For underwater photography, it is vital to have clear water—yet this is almost impossible to find. In working with swimming pools, one can add chemicals that assist in settling the fine particles of dust. In the ocean, one needs to go to far-away places. Pictures have a tendency to be blue underwater, particularly at a distance, so the best results are obtained when working as close to the subject as possible and using a red filter to neutralize the blue.

For underwater work, I carry an underwater meter and depend on it for my exposure.

To create this image, Diane swam straight at the camera, letting bubbles escape through her nose. Her hair flowed back, away from her face as she approached. When she slowed, it flared out.

Diane Webber, 1955

Diane Webber, 1955

FLOATING

How can Diane float on the surface in a diagonal position and still keep herself centered and her legs and feet from sinking? We solved this by stretching two lengths of monofilament fishing lines across the pool, held by one assistant on each side.

The only lighting used was natural sunlight. Sparkly reflections from the sun are seen in upper left, while a dif-ferent type of pattern on bottom right is made by the water moving against the curved bottom of the pool.

I prefer models to be posed on a diagonal. The slight S-curve is also pleasing to the artist's eye. By pointing her toes and extending her right arm, Diane was able to add another seven or eight inches to the total length of her body.

How can Diane float on the surface in a diagonal position and still keep herself centered and her legs and feet from sinking?

Brooke Mills

A FAVORITE MODEL

I was fortunate to meet a young woman like Brooke—who was a dancer and actress, as well as a model with perfect features and a beautiful body. Her main profession was acting, and she once told me that she was typecast—she had been the victim of murder in a dozen movies.

I think I was one of only two photographers who took partial nudes of her. She was not interested in photography for men's magazines. Brooke had a natural and relaxed attitude toward nudity. I first photographed her as a dancer in my studio, and then on the beach.

While doing a series of pictures in clothing for our stock photo catalog, Brooke mentioned she needed a new portrait. Wanting to avoid the standard, seated pose, I had her recline on a white paper background on the studio floor and swirled her thick, auburn tresses around her head, framing her face on one side. I used a ladder to have the vantage point directly above her and aimed the 72" Larson Reflectasol directly onto her face. I shot the image on a Hasselblad with a 150mm Sonar lens.

While doing a series of pictures in clothing for our stock photo catalog, Brooke mentioned she needed a new portrait.

Brooke Mills, 1971

This picture was taken by my wife, Alice, who is usually offering suggestions on the side, while I am concentrating on technical aspects. I was taking a picture of Brooke from a front view, using two light sources; one from a window at camera right, and a flood from camera left that fell on her shoulder. Alice was standing at the side, seeing Brooke's profile. She suddenly yelled, "Stop! Hand me the Pentax!" And because she is not usually so bossy, I figured she had something special. She did. **The effect of the side light on Brooke's expression was something I probably would have missed**, not having eyes that can observe oblique angles!

Seeing Brooke's profile, she suddenly yelled, "Stop! Hand me the Pentax!"

Brooke Mills, 1971

A client seeking pictures to illustrate a particular lighting system liked the photographs I had taken of Brooke. He wanted me to capture her in a series of poses that would result in a high-contrast, grainy effect.

Black and white 35mm film with an ASA speed of 1000 was used to increase the grain. I underexposed slightly and intensified the negatives by bleaching them and redeveloping the film in DK50. **This brought the negatives back to a normal looking exposure but doubled the grain.**

All poses were hard-lighted with two 1000 watt lights one above the other, behind two Larson 36" diffusion screens. A photo flood was placed on the background, and I made sure that it didn't strike Brooke's body by placing gobos between the light and her body.

Brooke's hair played a major part in many of the photographs. Its healthy quality and Brooke's ability to work with it helped tremendously. Here, Alice assisted in arranging the wavy strands once Brooke had it wrapped around her arms.

> He wanted me to capture her in a series of poses that would result in a high-contrast, grainy effect.

GRAIN

CANDID ATTITUDE

I was aiming for a lighter background on the dark side of Brooke's figure and a darker one on the light side. We achieved this by using two lights. One light was placed to camera right (to the side of Brooke's body), lighting the front of her torso while leaving her right arm and side in shadow and the background dark. **Another light, to camera left, was aimed at the background, shedding no light on her body.**

The hat was a replica of an old fashioned sunbonnet. Designer Jo Lathwood made it for me. You've seen it in other pictures of mine. It's come in handy with my nude studies because I like mixing a touch of the old with the new. I liked the candid attitude of Brooke's face, barely seen, and her attention on her clothing rather than looking into the camera.

The photograph was taken with 1000 speed film using the 35mm Pentax and an 85mm lens.

I liked the candid attitude of Brooke's face, barely seen.

Brooke Mills, 1971

122

OFF BALANCE

One light was placed high at camera right. A second light was directed at the background from camera left.

Being a dancer as well as an actress, Brooke comes up with poses that are quite original. This one, featuring her long hair, almost threw her off balance and caused her to break out in a long laugh.

This one almost threw her off balance.

Brooke Mills, 1971

Other Books from
Amherst Media™

Build Your Own Home Darkroom

Lista Duren & Will McDonald

This classic book teaches you how to build a high quality, inexpensive darkroom in your basement, spare room, or almost anywhere. Includes valuable information on: darkroom design, woodworking, tools, and more! $17.95 list, 8½x11, 160p, 50 photos, many illustrations, order no. 1092.

Into Your Darkroom Step by Step

Dennis P. Curtin

This is the ideal beginning darkroom guide. Easy to follow and fully illustrated each step of the way. Includes information on: the equipment you'll need, setup, making proof sheets and much more! $17.95 list, 8½x11, 90p, hundreds of photos, order no. 1093.

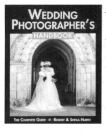

Wedding Photographer's Handbook

Robert and Sheila Hurth

A complete step-by-step guide to succeeding in the world of wedding photography. Packed with shooting tips, equipment lists, must-get photo lists, business strategies, and much more! $24.95 list, 8½x11, 176p, index, 100 b&w and color photos, diagrams, order no. 1485.

Outdoor and Location Portrait Photography

Jeff Smith

Learn how to work with natural light, select locations, and make clients look their best. Step-by-step discussions and helpful illustrations teach you the techniques you need to shoot outdoor portraits like a pro! $29.95 list, 8½x11, 128p, 60+ b&w and color photos, index, order no. 1632.

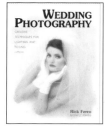

Wedding Photography: Creative Techniques for Lighting and Posing, 2nd Edition

Rick Ferro

Creative techniques for lighting and posing wedding portraits that will set your work apart from the competition. Covers every phase of wedding photography. $29.95 list, 8½x11, 128p, full color photos, index, order no. 1649.

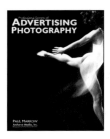

Professional Secrets of Advertising Photography

Paul Markow

No-nonsense information for those interested in the business of advertising photography. Includes: how to catch the attention of art directors, make the best bid, and produce the high-quality images your clients demand. $29.95 list, 8½x11, 128p, 80 photos, index, order no. 1638.

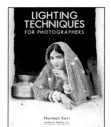

Lighting Techniques for Photographers

Norman Kerr

This book teaches you to predict the effects of light in the final image. It covers the interplay of light qualities, as well as color compensation and manipulation of light and shadow. $29.95 list, 8½x11, 120p, 150+ color and b&w photos, index, order no. 1564.

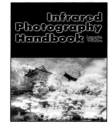

Infrared Photography Handbook

Laurie White

Covers black and white infrared photography: focus, lenses, film loading, film speed rating, batch testing, paper stocks, and filters. Black & white photos illustrate how IR film reacts. $29.95 list, 8½x11, 104p, 50 b&w photos, charts & diagrams, order no. 1419.

Infrared Nude Photography

Joseph Paduano

A stunning collection of images with how-to text that teaches how to shoot the infrared nude. Shot on location in natural settings, including the Grand Canyon, Bryce Canyon and the New Jersey Shore. $29.95 list, 8½x11, 96p, over 50 photos, order no. 1080.

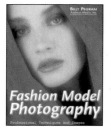

Fashion Model Photography

Billy Pegram

For the photographer interested in shooting commercial model assignments, or working with models to create portfolios. Includes techniques for dramatic composition, posing, selection of clothing, and more! $29.95 list, 8½x11, 120p, 58 photos, index, order no. 1640.

Achieving the Ultimate Image

Ernst Wildi

Ernst Wildi teaches the techniques required to take world class, technically flawless photos. Features: exposure, metering, the Zone System, composition, evaluating an image, and more! $29.95 list, 8½x11, 128p, 120 b&w and color photos, index, order no. 1628.

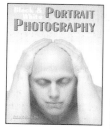

Black & White Portrait Photography

Helen T. Boursier

Make money with b&w portrait photography. Learn from top b&w shooters! Studio and location techniques, with tips on preparing your subjects, selecting settings and wardrobe, lab techniques, and more! $29.95 list, 8½x11, 128p, 130+ photos, index, order no. 1626

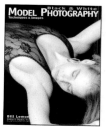

Black & White Model Photography

Bill Lemon

Create dramatic sensual images of nude and lingerie models. Explore lighting, setting, equipment use, posing and composition with the author's discussion of 60 unique images. $29.95 list, 8½x11, 128p, 60 b&w photos and illustrations, index, order no. 1577.

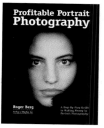

Profitable Portrait Photography

Roger Berg

A step-by-step guide to making money in portrait photography. Combines information on portrait photography with detailed business plans to form a comprehensive manual for starting or improving your business. $29.95 list, 8½x11, 104p, 100 photos, index, order no. 1570

Professional Secrets for Photographing Children

Douglas Allen Box

Covers every aspect of photographing children on location and in the studio. Prepare children and parents for the shoot, select the right clothes, capture a child's personality, and shoot storytelling themes. $29.95 list, 8½x11, 128p, 74 photos, index, order no. 1635.

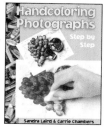

Handcoloring Photographs Step-by-Step

Sandra Laird & Carey Chambers

Learn to handcolor photographs step-by-step with the new standard in handcoloring reference books. Covers a variety of coloring media and techniques with plenty of colorful photographic examples. $29.95 list, 8½x11, 112p, 100+ color and b&w photos, order no. 1543.

Swimsuit Model Photography

Cliff Hollenbeck

The complete guide to the business of swimsuit model photography. Includes: finding and working with models, selecting equipment, posing, using props and backgrounds, and more! $29.95 list, 8½x11, 112p, over 100 b&w and color photos, index, order no. 1605.

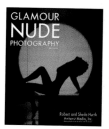

Glamour Nude Photography, *revised*

Robert and Sheila Hurth

Create stunning nude images! The Hurths guide you through selecting models, choosing locations, lighting, and shooting techniques. Includes: posing, equipment, makeup and hairstyles, and more! $29.95 list, 8½x11, 128p, over 100 b&w and color photos, index, order no. 1499.

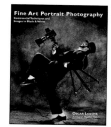

Fine Art Portrait Photography

Oscar Lozoya

The author examines a selection of his best photographs, and provides detailed technical information about how he created each. Lighting diagrams accompany each photograph. $29.95 list, 8½x11, 128p, 58 photos, index, order no. 1630.

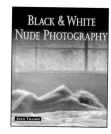

Black & White Nude Photography

Stan Trampe

This book teaches the essentials for beginning fine art nude photography. Includes info on finding your first model, selecting equipment, and scenarios of a typical shoot, plus more! Includes 60 photos taken with b&w and infrared films. $24.95 list, 8½x11, 112p, index, order no. 1592.

The Art of Portrait Photography

Michael Grecco

Michael Grecco reveals the secrets behind his dramatic portraits which have appeared in magazines such as *Rolling Stone* and *Entertainment Weekly*. Includes: lighting, posing, creative development, and more! $29.95 list, 8½x11, 128p, 60 photos, order no. 1651.

Photographer's Guide to Polaroid Transfer

Christopher Grey

Step-by-step instructions make it easy to master Polaroid transfer and emulsion lift-off techniques and add new dimensions to your photographic imaging. Fully illustrated every step of the way to ensure good results the very first time! $29.95 list, 8½x11, 128p, 50 photos, order no. 1653.

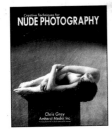

Creative Techniques for Nude Photography

Christopher Grey

Create dramatic fine art portraits of the human figure in black & white. Features studio techniques for posing, lighting, working with models, creative props and backdrops. Also includes ideas for shooting outdoors. $29.95 list, 8½x11, 128p, 60 incredible b&w photos, order no. 1655.

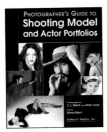

Photographer's Guide to Shooting Model & Actor Portfolios

CJ Elfont, Edna Elfont and Alan Lowy

Learn to create outstanding images for actors and models looking for work in fashion, theater, television, or the big screen. Includes the business, photographic and professional information you need to succeed! $29.95 list, 8½x11, 128p, 100 photos, order no. 1659.

Creative Lighting Techniques for Studio Photographers

Dave Montizambert

Master studio lighting and gain complete creative control over your images. Whether you are shooting portraits, cars, tabletop or any other subject, Dave Montizambert teaches you the skills you need to confidently create with light. $29.95 list, 8½x11, 120p, 80+ photos, order no. 1666

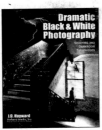

Dramatic Black & White Photography:
Shooting and Darkroom Techniques

J.D. Hayward

Create dramatic fine-art images with the master b&w techniques in this book. From outstanding lighting techniques to top-notch, creative darkroom work, this book takes b&w to the next level! $29.95 list, 8½x11, 128p, order no. 1687.

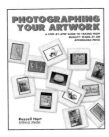

Photographing Your Artwork

Russell Hart

A step-by-step guide for taking high-quality slides of artwork for submission to galleries, magazines, grant committees, etc. Learn the best photographic techniques to make your artwork (be it 2D or 3D) look its very best! $29.95 list, 8½x11, 128p, 80 b&w photos, order no. 1688.

Posing and Lighting Techniques for Studio Photographers

J.J. Allen

Master the skills needed for beautiful lighting for portraits of any subject. Posing techniques for flattering, classic images help turn every portrait into a work of art. $29.95 list, 8½x11, 120p, 125 full-color photos, order no. 1697.

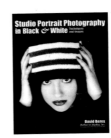

Studio Portrait Photography in Black & White

David Derex

From concept to presentation, you'll learn how to select clothes, create beautiful lighting, prop and pose top-quality black & white portraits in the studio. $29.95 list, 8½x11, 128p, 70 photos, order no. 1689.

Corrective Lighting and Posing Techniques for Portrait Photographers

Jeff Smith

Learn to make every client look his or her best by using lighting and posing to conceal real or imagined flaws—from baldness, to acne, to figure flaws. $29.95 list, 8½x11, 120p, full color, 150 photos, order no. 1711.

Make-Up Techniques for Photography

Cliff Hollenbeck

Step-by-step text paired with photographic illustrations teach you the art of photographic make-up. Learn to make every portrait subject look his or her best with great styling techniques for black & white or color photography. $29.95 list, 8½x11, 120p, 80 full color photos, order no. 1704.

More Photo Books Are Available

Write or fax for a *FREE* catalog:
AMHERST MEDIA
PO BOX 586
AMHERST, NY 14226 USA

Fax: 716-874-4508

www.AmherstMedia.com

Ordering & Sales Information:

INDIVIDUALS: If possible, purchase books from an Amherst Media retailer. Write to us for the dealer nearest you. To order direct, send a check or money order with a note listing the books you want and your shipping address. U.S. & overseas freight charges are $3.50 for the first book, and $1.00 for each additional book. Visa and Master Card accepted. New York state residents add 8% sales tax.

DEALERS, DISTRIBUTORS & COLLEGES: Write, call or fax to place orders. For price information, contact Amherst Media or an Amherst Media sales representative. Net 30 days.

All prices, publication dates, and specifications are subject to change without notice.

Prices are in U.S. dollars. Payment in U.S. funds only.